*Est. 2019*

# *The*
# *Poetry*
# *Book II*

*By*
*Ramsey Wake*

For more information about permission to reproduce
selections from this book email to
ramseywake@gmail.com

Or.. don't reproduce my shit, make your own.. lazy
ass

Manufacturing by Bubba
Book design by Luca

ISBN: 978-0-359-90118-0

Content ID:

Produced by The Wake Poetry Corporation
(Not a real corporation yet, but a guy can dream)

One day we'll have a website link here:

And a business address here:

For all social media viewers and for business
contacting:
Not this Christmas

A bad joke for those of you still here

Poetry,
Sentences and words
Put together
By hitting the enter key
At key moments.


Now..
Let's Begin

a return to the deepest marks in my
mind,
a chance to learn something
or a last chance opportunity to try
and find
what you've been hiding deep inside
i hope to the best of my capabilities
that something beautiful gets stuck
in your memory..


screw this, it's just an intro you
don't need poetry shoved down your
throat here. i do sincerely hope
you'll get something out of this, a
feeling, an undiscovered emotion,
some type of educational discovery.
because otherwise these are just more
words on more wasted paper. let's
strive to be better than that. let's
commit to being something better than
we are right now.
enjoy.

# Table of Contents

# Poetical Alphabet

**A**wkwardly he took his first steps
how beautiful the mind of a child
so oblivious to what comes next

**B**etween choosing something that cracks
or splatters
I'll take the latter
because in a perfectly painted wall
it's the scratches
that matter.

**C**reation, it does beg to ask the question
was there a creator and are we the grand
invention?
or does it speak to those
easily fooled by the others
with bad intention.

**D**efinition is bold white and bold black
vaguely made i am the shadow that hides,
for i am neither bolds
in both do i lack.

**E**rotic adventures and our bad teenage decisions
we surrender our bodies to bad tormentors
and permanent incisions.

**F**urious is a world enslaved by political
leaders
it pushes us to the brink of extinction
and offers a choice,
will you be proactive
or join the sleepers.

Gorgeous are those mountain peaks
to climb to the top is a reminder
that you're not one of the weak
but of the brave
the strong
the courageous,
even when considered outrageous.

Hope is your eyes and your smile
thank god for your existence,
for the last time i've seen hope
well,
it's been a while.

Intentional approachment sparking
unintentional relationship
the ones we most hang onto
are the ones that cause a power trip
a powerful dynamic
that shakes the bushes
with unbreakable grip.

Jobs remind us that we were meant to be
captive slaves
and that for a price we've broken,
we will live that way
until we dig our graves.

Kinda complicated
when you've fallen in love uncontrollably
she tells you she's in love with someone else..
probably,
but you hang onto the hope
she'll love you one day.
day by day
until the love you should've loved
passes away.

Look around you
can't you see the pain ?
everything around us is falling
are you insane ?
these mind games we play,
every trial of every day
these are my last words
my mind is lame.

Money drives society ?
so how can a broke man
develop such high notoriety.

Not a good person
he doesn't make sense.
perhaps if i viewed the world through his lens
then we could finally make amends.

Only a few mistakes
are mistakes that make or break
though not telling you i loved you,
now  body and soul
to take.

Probably the most preposterous pondering
to ever be pondered,
what is this world
and how much have we truly wandered.

Questions and rumors of a far away land,
where things are free
love is abundant
and life is grand.

Randomly placed into a segregated community
of  distasteful creatures
my flying colors stand out
like an excessively loud movie feature.

Searching for the island
that calls my name
the fallen youth gather here
all the same
they leave subtle hints
to solve this subtle game.

Treasure is buried
under pounds of sand
broken hearts are hidden
when covered by hand.

Unless you assume that shattered society
can fix itself on its own,
what are you doing to change it
besides moan and groan ?

Violence caused me the loss of an ear
i have to thank you
for now when you speak
i do not hear.

What we have lost in our past
can never be uncovered,
the only hope is the archaeologists
who know the path
for the rediscovered.

Xylophone plays thy gentle tune
sitting quietly, i listen
so thoroughly amused
i am four years old
with an ear for good news
this just in,
i've learned something new.

Years of fighting have pushed us to our brink
years of fighting
never dying
saving ourselves before we sink,
now i'm home
and there's nothing i can say
nothing i can do
just drink.

Zippers run
from north to south
cloudtops overhead
beckon me to shout
hurricanes approaching
turn back around.

# THE WILD RETURNS

do you dream of the far away ?
of lands not yet discovered
feelings not yet felt ?
do you feel grossly underestimated ?
like the world doesn't notice
what change you are presenting
are you considered crazy ?
are you actually crazy ?
if you sit here
and you feel different from normality,
normality is a fantasy
being crazy is the new fancy.
and here we can dream together
of a wilderness that supports our will,
to become eternal
to become forever
to become truly wild

## Episode One: A Wild Sight

look up
soaring high above the mountains
far beyond a birds capabilities,
flies a man
and he calls.
look down
far below the depths reachable
by the deepest sea creatures,
swimming is a man
and he calls.
look all around
for there are different people everywhere
though faces can be seen
on different placements
in similar ways
it's the eyes that can't change.
the eyes,
they call
they sing
they ball
they tell stories of broken hearts
and dreams that never came true.
they say 'we're through with trying to look
average'
it's time to take a stand
and stand up to the status quo
we are calling to the wild.
for answers to questions
pertaining to ourselves
about why we've been beaten
and broken
we've been looking for a reason.
about why our reasoning
is so undeniably different from others
why others look at us with eyes
that don't shine back.
we are seeking something,
something to show us the specialist
built inside our bones.
the altercation in our genetics,
the random chance changes in our dna,

all of these equations point to a solution
far greater than common mind comprehension.
a wild predicament
a catastrophe on legs
it's a soul
who seeks uncommon things

## Episode Two: This Evening

Today
i am writing to my notebook
my trustworthy friend
my open ear
my thought tracker.
today has been catastrophic
and shines a bright spotlight
on my blemishes and failures,
i am reminded that my cheeks
don't feel right when they aren't wet
my soul only knows what's numb,
my ears have become common to quiet.
i am actively seeking a sedative
to make my mind
shut the fuck up
so i can find peace
for just a few moments.
i am broken
and my cure doesn't exist
i am disease
inside of flesh
i am poison
trapped in a cup,
and here on this evening
a smile never dares
cross my face
words never make their way
to my lips
and my toes don't reach
for another inch,
all force was concentrated on breathing
gasping for air
my lungs were giving
such little effort.
when everyone forgets who you are
what you're capable of
you feel incapable
handicapped
and incomplete.
though the sun begins to set
and the sky breaks into colors of pink and blue

i am reminded that my stone pathway
leads to a house in the forest
where my broken soul is rooted amongst the big
trees
the biggest of them all.
and a smile won't reach my face today
or tomorrow
maybe not for a week
but a season is coming,
where i will dance
until the hour is late
i will sing with the birds
till even they
can't take my song
i will love until nature loves me back.
on this evening
i will look forward to the life
i will love to live
a life of wild crazy stories

## Episode Three: the dogs sitting on the couch, im laying on the floor (chewing a bone)

Ode to a world being backward
let chaos reign.
let things flip
until they've flopped
like a bare belly
and a pool's water top.
have you ever seen human teeth
gnawing viciously against bone ?
grinding and chewing
gaining self satisfaction in the process ?
he only eats
when papa dog says he can
he only gets fresh air when somebody opens the
door
its enough to survive
but as any human wonders
can i be more than a slaving pet,
who's life's agenda is mapped out
before even being born ?
many live their life
unobservant to their cage
yet people who don't even know your name
or your face
have arranged you college plans
that lead to student debt
that leads to a full time job
that carries you till retirement
that you ride hopefully
for the rest of your life.
go outside when i tell you
eat food when i let you
chew your bone
and never
jump on the couch.
but why are they so afraid
for you to enter onto
the large cushion seats ?

it's a sign of rebellion
a sign that the system can be broken
like a doggy door
a self replenishing food dish
a floor covered in shit.
this world is on fire
and stays perfectly calm
as in cannibalistic fashion
it eats what little it hasn't contaminated,
this place we call home
is only as self sustaining as those
who inhabit its soil
we have messily torched our trees
and covered it in layers of concrete
like a burial of mother nature.
how lazy we've become
as if our goal is to move
as little as possible
to be as safe as possible
to be as close to others as we can
with as little interaction we can manage
how well do you know your neighbor ?
we are so far from what we knew
and have forgotten that the past
isn't always a wrong answer
deceived into always looking forward
forgetting that we are pulling roots
that are not so easily put back in place
like you cannot so easily glue back together
a human sawed in half
our dominance is the dominant depressant
in a domino effect to destroy
the destiny of humankind.
but my opinion is irrelevant.
i am crazier than the craziest cockatoo
flying through a firework display
hell my dog sits on the couch,
i lay on the ground
and chew
on my hand crafted bone.
i may be crazy
but who's to say who is what
what have you made for yourself recently ?

it wouldn't be a wild guess to assume
not much

# Episode Four: Let It Fly

when i say i don't feel fear
i am lying
i am fearful of failing
i am fearful that i won't be loved
or accepted.
i fear the rapids
and the close proximity to the waterfall
i fear its drop
i am scared
to continue paddling towards my certain death,
and even more terrified
of trying to paddle away from it
because it's when you turn your back to the
world
that it grabs you
and pulls you down again
and beats your stomach blue.
but to look them in the eye,
and take the beating of brutal blows
to the forehead and cheeks
until your face feels more like rubber
and less like the place
you hold things dear.
i am scared of the mountain
though so many have climbed its peak before me
i cannot help but imagine my falling
my failing.
though it's only when i come to realize
that my falling is so separate from failing
for when i fall
the wind does not judge me,
my velocity and trajectories
don't mock me,
my views are unparalleled.
and even if i die
it's not to the beaten and bloody hands
of my closest friends
it's not from my family's feet
breaking my beak
it wasn't my enemies

pointing out my informality
i just fell.
or
i flew temporarily
and if my life is mine to live
than i am to conquer what fears
haven't been defeated
and i shouldn't stop
until they've been depleted.
so my life's direction should be direct
not looking for squabbles
and not avoiding those things
that blockade my potentials,
for nobody can break a fear free
but yourself.
don't let life live
do life well
and then you can let it fly
wildly

# Episode Five: No Masks on These Paths

recently i find myself
doing a lot of things that aren't me,
i say things to some
that i don't feel inside
simply to appease them
i'd be a sore liar if i didn't admit
that war has begun in my spirit
it is not of my character
to be the people person,
but when your true character
gives forth the opportunity
to be in good standing with others
it's hard to remember the cost
you're paying.
your genuineness
your uniqueness
your enoughness
these are untradeables.
your mannerisms
the nature in which you speak
and the way in which you display love
these are non-negotiables,
it's time to stop selling stock
and stop investing
into what you believe is the way
you are received
it's time to stop caring
how you're perceived.
you're worth more than
others' dreams of yourself
you'll never truly be happy with mimicking,
what you've learned
works well for others.
the truth is even if others treat you
like they want you to act a certain way
they'd appreciate you more as yourself,
and if they don't
they aren't worth the worry.
the best you is the you
that you already are,

and the one
you always will be.
no matter how large the mask you wear
it is still just a mask
no matter what clothes you bear
they are just clothes
no matter how you speak
those are just lost words
and lost opportunities
to say things you really wanted to say
the sooner you start finding yourself
the sooner you can be happy in your skin.
and i'm not saying it's magic
and i'm not saying it'll work overnight
though i will say
the path in the right direction
can't be walked in the shoes you wear
because people tell you to wear them.
it must be your shoes
and the mask must go too
this path is wild,
but what other kind of life is there
for people like us..
it's in our title

# Episode Six: Mountain Chasers

no peak too high to climb
no road too far to drive
i will see all i can in this life.

what could possibly be the point to this place
?
could it be that we are all here
to gather wealth
and wage wars
in hopes to be named
the greatest race ?
i say no
i say there's no chance,
if it is me you're asking
we're here to adventure
we're here to discover
we're here to try.
and we can't try
by sitting idle in an average home
with an average job
helping an average economy
stay average.
when does the bar get pushed
in that scenario ?
when can you stand at the award ceremony
and say "yes i did that,
yes i broke through that"
that too
would be the reason for life
to break through
every constraint you cross,
the path to freedom
isn't physically geographed
it's a metaphysical mountain,
it's a mental range of peaks
that puts the appalachians to shame
it makes nepal look flat.
some peaks you can't even grasp
as you begin your climb
this is enough to make those
who are weak stay at home

not even dare to continue,
some will lose their minds
as they begin their climbs,
some have already dug themselves
into such deep and dark holes
that they spend their lives
trying to get out of the sinkhole
and never even find the mountain
that stops their freedom.
but there are a few,
there is us
the wild
who climb the first peak..
and find out
it's only just a hill
a small test
and then
another small hill
and another
and another.
as you tackle each hill
you let yourself go
more and more,
you feel a skip
in the common step
now you're dancing from each hilltop
excited to climb
to its point.
and by the time you come across a big mountain
it doesnt matter its size,
you've been training for this
little by little your legs got stronger
now this bigger peak,
something you would have never climbed before,
is a beautiful challenge
and sure
a mental blockade is enough to disturb
even the strongest of us
but will it break you
is the question.
you may take longer breaks
on this scramble to the peak,
you may take frequent looks behind you

and weigh your options
you may lose your breath.
but if determination
fills your blood vessels
and the challenge of this peak
encourages you to accomplish it
then you have the eyes
of those who can beat anything.
for the best mountain chaser
isn't chasing mountains at all
they are chasing a dream,
but when a mountain comes around
they smile
get wild
dig deep
and climb

# Episode Seven: Hide and I'll Go Seek

to the earth
i've prepared a challenge,
hide.
hide your greatest beauties
bury them deep in the ruins
have them disappear from
the works of internet searches
and have them scratched from maps,
place thick fog around their surroundings
deem them cursed by locals
cover them in snow and sand.
i'll be your seeker
give me routes yet traveled
take me to places that don't exist
where even a compass
considers himself lost,
abstract places where maps depict blank
emptiness.
trust me
dear beautiful planet
i'm not here to destroy your relics,
my adventures are not in the name
to destroy your true historical beauty
through half believable stories
vacation resorts
new civilizations,
not even my photos
will reach your highest grandeur
in those moments i will refrain from my camera
for i know of honor,
to be shown something so spectacular,
those who deserve will see
and it's not fit for the others.
so hide
hide
hide.
and i'll hike
and drive
and traverse until im gray and old.
and i behold all your wild beauty.

## Episode Eight: Lovers of Broken Things

there are some,
some who see the world differently
some who chose their own
life filter
and turn down the automatic preset
offered to them.
these someone's
are broken,
these someone's
take the scrap
and disfigured pieces
from once unique creations
and try their best
to piece them back together.
we know why they broke apart
hell we saw how it happened
some of us were even the assholes
who dropped these creations
from the buildings
hysterically laughing as they
crashed and combusted.
these killers of character
have clawed their way to a point
on top of the others,
they sit in the crows nest
looking down
laughing at those
who are falling
and getting up
and falling again.
but they only get to sit
in their comfortable nest
as long as the tree
doesn't shake too hard
it's when the wind chimes sing
and leaves start rustling
that these killers get quiet.
we are the wind
we have love for those who are trying,

and we who are trying
all banded together as one
can perform hurricane level performances..
you may call it disastrous art.
but it takes all,
not one or a few
not some or a couple
at the very least
a lot,
this world would love nothing more
than to take your paintings by the hand
and knife them through their core
for no reason more
than to see your baby become breathless,
to see terror rip across
your pale face
if only they realized that
you're making a masterpiece,
you're making something you love
you're committing effort.
but people have a way of seeing
what they feel is missing,
those who are blank at heart
use your canvas of expression to exercise
their imaginations of what would bring
the world mass satisfaction.
and when you express anything short of their
expectations
as you always will
you are met by killers.
but if you were plugged into the wind,
and as a movement
the crows nest was launched from the tree
that killer becomes nothing more than a bird
and you are an act of dramatic motion
a chaotic commotion.
stand tall
stand as one
and pick up your starving
and wild brother
who isn't able to stand yet.

# Episode Nine - Calm Waters

we seem to seek the choppy life
the life of fast pace and energy
the good life.
we chase after happiness
so fast that we forget
it's when we slow down
that we have time
to smile at nothing,
everyone loves a big wave
a catastrophic event
that occurs before your eyes
and yet doesn't affect you
in the slightest
besides possibly a little spray,
they scream passion
they instill fear
and they seek beauty.
yet nobody ever mentions
the calmer wave
the wave that didn't capsize the small boat
the wave that didn't make an angry crash
a wave that subtly rolled into the beachside
seemingly so happy with his short life.
and life is short
so who would you rather aspire to be
to live big ?
to be considered
high and mighty ?
to be eye catching ?
but to sacrifice living peace to chaos.
or to be a calm rolling wave
to never harm
to never chase fame
but to live life in your own quiet lane.
to be a piece of harmony
or to be an orchestrator of chaos,
both lives can be wild
neither life has to be the wrong answer,
but statistically speaking it's safe to assume
that you would prefer one or the other.

cheers to whoever you are
and your further understanding
of who you want to be,
a roar
or a smile

# Episode Ten - More Than Wild

droplets slide down your shoulders
and the brim of your nose
you don't move.
the smell of wet pine and cedar
fill your brain with peace
the air so pure
so fresh
all you can do is exhale
and close your eyes
some moments aren't meant to end,
like any moment you're looking out at an
oceanscape
or the mountains of the cascades.
though we don't live in society's reality
our reality is true that not many of us
can be wild all of the time,
we all have wild in us
but most will only find it possible
to call upon that wild spirit
on occasion.
so this one is to you reader
you who still lives in society
but is living in your own reality
you must learn,
learn how to become
more than just wild
learn how to be yourself
in society
for that's just as wild
as this wild culture
we dream of in these books.
for if you dress how you want
you smile when you'd like
you dance anywhere and everywhere at anytime
and you love who you love then,
just then,
will the wild drip its way into common society
and though we turn our backs
and spit at those who call us insane
for believing in something different,

there are those
who see our new take on world perception
and may just feel something
that was buried deep
spark up inside.
maybe they begin to test
what has been taught
maybe they become wild too,
or maybe they don't
but they still break the system's chains
in their own way
and i will always support that,
all of these possibilities
possibilities are only rational
by taking a chance on something
previously imagined as irrational
i'm currently realizing this fact more than
ever before
so i dare you to take a chance on something
i dare you to stand out
i dare you to dance in the streets
i dare you to break every system you cross
even my own.
don't just do wild
become more than it
discover glory in changing the world
and in saving it.
be more than wild
be you.

# NewKeepers

Since the fall of the peacekeepers
life as we know it has succumbed to an
apocalyptic state.
free spirits spirited around every town of
every state and instead of joining forces,
partaking in war was the choice they made.
for any sole is not equally measured in
freeness
nor in wild nature.
the world prepares for downfall
body counts grow higher by the second
another one downed
and another.
out of the darkness shines a new light with an
old face
a ragtag group of peacekeeper groupies
and they're ready to take on the world.
they are here with a message
"we are lovers, not born to fight"
we naturally collide
but the dead
with the blood on knuckles and knives
that is not how things should be.
they are chasing beauty
color
and light.
they are the new keepers
and they are love
despite the hardened faces they show,
it's an impossible road they are trying to walk
trying to fix the world as just a few.
but they have something we all lack
since colors faded and all went black.
passion
furious passion
and nothing
stands between passion
and its goals

## Agitator

let the buzzers buzz beautifully
buttons are being pressed tonight.
let the ragers rage ragefully
for i don't care if your anger is enough to be
violent
violence is meant to be violated
viciously by vacant fists
of which i possess a pair of.
i live my life to make sure you fume over
i love tapping your boiling points
every time you melt over
i have the clarification that your confidence
is confirmed a waste of time
and you are just like everyone else.
there is nothing
more agitating
than the agitator,
but if there was a second
it would be the average,
these liars who pretend
life is perfect
pretend they have peace
fake having a smile
they can't afford to place on their face.
smiling isn't cheap
and if you wear what you can't afford
eventually you'll go broke.
you wonder why you're always taking deep
breaths
it's quite obvious
you haven't tasted fresh air in a while.
your stresses,
look at the bigger fucking picture
the question of how much milk and eggs you have
left
shouldn't steal breath
you're just being a first class shithead.
but now you've agitated this poor old agitator
and don't expect me to put my hands into a
furnace

and come out cold
and don't expect this raging fire to silence
there's only escalation from here on out
there's only more buttons needing pressing,
how many more do you have left ?
if you can count only a few
you must be dreaming
it sounds like you could use some agitation.

## Silhouette Twins

in this dark gothic function
all we know is the nightmares,
those cold long nights
wide awake
fending off the lies
drowning out the voices.
i am just a civilian
and im not yet ready to fight the villains that
control my city
the villains that oppress me
for i can't fight for myself until i understand
why i'm worth fighting for,
i have abilities
i just don't know what they do.
then jumping from mountain top to mountain top
a silhouette moves along
with a swift move of incomprehensible boldness,
i run for the mountains.
to my unexpected capability
the cold didn't kill me
the altitude didn't disturb anything
but the voices saying i shouldn't and couldn't.
i reached the peak
a few peaks over sat the silhouette
i took the jump
and landed on the next peak.
and again and again
until the silhouette noticed my jumping
and she jumped to meet me
the most beautiful
no longer a silhouette.
eyes that were welcoming
a small form whose heart was almost as big as
she was,
and a smile that could make even the people who
feel least important feel like they matter.
"may i jump with you?"
i asked
"only if you can keep up."
the sweet voice said
and with a wink she was off

as we jumped
the villains fled from my city.
for they knew upon my return
I would be more powerful than any plan they
could conjure
more powerful than brute strength or mental
trickery
i was enlightened by the silhouette
now i too can jump on my enemies
and i don't have to do it alone
for i have found my silhouette twin.

# The Monster

it's on this day i have come to fully
understand
that we will never fully understand each other
in our world force fields stand taller than
your average giant,
religious viewsets more complicated than zeus
marrying the virgin mary,
and the priest presiding over the wedding was
buddha.
communication shut down like a solicitor trying
to talk to the president about his sex life,
i guess i was just neive
to think you and i could ever breath the same
air without tension pressing into each other's
lungs
i guess i'm just a little unaware
to dream that we could manage our way through
our indifference.
i guess i'm just a little bit lame
to truly believe that if i drove from
northernmost washington
and stopped in the middlemost oregon
that you'd take the drive from california to
meet me in the middle.
you never compromised
and i never took the drive
a barrier of movement,
a wind more powerful than all the earth's
largest hurricanes pushed my body away from the
car
my brain away from my body
and my body away from my soul.
and now this monster of a creation
this monster that's so done with playing
imitation
is just about ready
to take his vacation into permanent imagination
out of desperation with his infatuation of a
life lived free of limitation.

these were the last of days
for this dying monster i thought
but along came a girl
so small and care free
whistling and happy
such a wondrous sight to see.
even a monster like me
could understand that she is the face of peace
"follow me monster thing"
the little voice spoke
and so i did
and away we went
perhaps even the scariest figure
has purpose to the smallest of people

# Girl Wonder

a mere shadow of her striking boy brother
though she held values so much higher than he
she cared for nature and learning to live
carefree.
she sought out simplicity and elegance
leaving behind the city and all its irrelevance
she was unhappy living in a city locked by
gates which were guarded by gatekeepers,
from inside she could smell the fresh air
calling to her
telling her of far away worlds
that had forests and rivers and mountains
beasts and happy faces and even monsters.
she escaped and vowed to return to the city
to save those who couldn't smell the air she
could,
she promised to change the minds of the
gatekeepers
without hurting anyone or anything.
so on the day she met the monster
and told him he still had reason to be a
monstrosity,
she told him there stood a city that was
controlled diabolically
he spoke of someone he knew would help
an old friend
a real angry fellow
always agitated and never mellow.
so they searched out the agitator who called
them liars, cheaters,
and killers
"you cheaters of reality
killers of aristocracy
and liars of all in this virtuality
i am here emphatically,
together we will end the gatekeepers."
watching from beyond were a pair
standing side by side
something truly rare
in lightning like speed they sped down the
mountain to where the group was gathered

"this, is a team"
"and with this team
we can fulfill  this dream"

# Gatekeepers

to hell with the dreamers
those ruined souls
those feeble hearted children
those weak minded things.
it's my vow
to ensure they never cross my gates
to ensure my city remains great
and to ensure
that the dreamers stop dreaming.
for it's their dreams
that stop proper progress,
dreaming of improving things
that aren't to be meddled with.
they are fools
they are unteachable
they are unreachable
but with my gates in place
they are killable.
a dreamer can only go
so long out there
having no ability
to dream amongst others.
they will rot
become insane
and die away like the trees who fall
and nobody hears them say
"i must rest"
the death of the dreamers is imperative,
it's a necessity
it means that the commonwealth
and the common folk can live forever
they live in harmonious repetition.
for the only thing that can damage our
practices
is creative influence,
so i raise my gates high
and i watch from the walls
no dreamer would dare to come cross me.

# The War for The City

freeing this city without death would be oh so
hard,
stealth was a known necessity amongst the
group.
the silhouettes used their mountain jumping to
clear the gates so quietly in the night,
the monster who carried girl wonder scaled the
wall as silently as he could,
while the agitator stood in front of the gates
arms crossed.
guns and red dots crossed his chest more times
than a few,
"do you mean to pass our gates ?"
"pass them ? i mean to destroy them.
i am stronger than your strongest fighter,
i am the agitator fucker
and i will not go quietly..
but my friends will."
monster and the silhouette twins with a quick
sweep snatched the gatekeepers of their
weapons,
now defenseless and stunned by the monster
standing as tall as their gates,
they were forced into surrender.
once they were escorted out of their towers and
off their gates,
monster gave a small kick to the gate and
watched the whole thing fall with a clang.
this was the shortest take over to ever take
place.
the truth is,
those that keep us contained aren't actually
all that powerful,
they just appear powerful by their high
positions,
but this city has nobody standing high any
longer..
besides monster of course.

# A City Restored

as people emerged from their rows of housing
they did not see the team
instead a large painting on the ground
a painting of a city
not so different from this
but with unique huts
and container homes
instead of suburbans.
with colors splattered on the walls
instead of black and white
with a clean lake
and newly planted trees
with no capital building
towering over top
and certainly not a gate
keeping others out
people of every species
all living together
even monsters.
the painting was so moving
many went back and torched their homes
in search of achieving this image
they were filled with a drive
to become even better than they are now
it didn't take long before the look was
achieved.
how beautiful they built
taking personal liberties where needed
to ensure their freedom from any restraints.
the city of freedom was finally built
and it smelled of fresh air.
the newkeepers were successful
and nobody will need to liberate this city
again

# My Name Is...

## Chapter I

you two leggers walk so weird
talk so weird
you two leggers eat how ?
you play how ?
by giving a guy a ball
and then tackle to get it back ?
oh
that actually sounds pretty fun
and though i am always up for a walk
and a few throws of a ball
my favorite time of day is after
when we go to bed,
and you scratch my favorite spots
with your delicate and gentle hands
you rub my sore muscles
and tell me how good i really am.
and through a look
just a simple gaze into your eyes
sometimes even a tail wag
i tell you how much i love you.
but i watch you two leggers
and i cringe
because with just one look
i can relay a message that's deeply powerful
and important
yet you say nonstop things
and most of them are unimportant.
once it's time to actually say something of
value,
you guys freeze
like when i wait for a treat to be thrown.
no initiative
so sensitive
so overthought
you think i know exactly where you're throwing
the ball ?

no !
i just react
you tell me where
and i go that way,
now if i don't want to
i simply don't.
so when my two legged caretaker
complains of being stuck in routines
that are unhealthy
i don't understand why he doesn't just
stop.
so many expectations in the two legged world
so many worries
and doubts
and fears
so much pity for being dealt a bad hand.
think about all the ball time you miss out on
because you're thinking about something
that hasn't even happened yet.
what i'm saying is
life could be more fun
if you spend less of it in the past
and not a penny more in the future
but more eyes fixed on the now.
also give more treats to us dogs
we like them.
oh and stop making us do those damn tricks
they're compromising my fun
Thanks.
-Dog

# Chapter II

you build me up
and i separate
these skinny halls
i create
without the windows and doors
i'm a closed world
ready to hide you away from troubles.
i've watched you cry
i've seen your struggles
you painted my sides
nailed memories to my thighs
i once carried paintings
you made when you were young
but like caterpillars become butterflies
i changed so you could thrive.
we are one in the same
i watched you grow up more than your parents
ever did
i was there when you first drank out of the
bottle
couldn't figure out how to open the lid
you vowed to never touch that toxin again
vowed it was a poisonous killer
a killer of men.
and you grew up
but your heritage
so filled with torturous belligerence
you couldn't help yourself
you said you needed some help.
bashed your fist into my stomach
forming a hole
a visual marker
to remind you of your violent nature.
your heart became cold
so bold you never listened to what you were
told,
now you're old
moving out into a world
filled with people who live on the curve
seeing where they came from
but not where they want to be.

and you will forget about me
for my display now stands as a reminder
of the road you're heading down
violent and angry.
i am now alone
waiting on hold for you to return
you surely will one day
when you're older and more mature.
until then i am abandoned and quiet
gathering dust
dancing in the silence.
my name is grey
and i am your wall

# Chapter III

i was formed at sea
with full intentions on making my big impact on
land.
it seems i'm only famous
if i bring my pain back to the surface
to the place where feet belong,
i'm not loved
im feared.
but i'm also mistaken
people look at me as if i was
a perfectly sculpted master mess
though that i am not,
i have no parents and therefore no genetic code
there was none before me
like me
there will be none after me
that are like me.
i am fully unique
i should be respectfully admired
i should be an inspiration.
i understand your response
to be that of disgust
i know that the path i walk
leaves a trail of destruction and dismay
but have you considered
that you're the one who built into my trail ?
maybe you made me into the monster
maybe i was a cultural phenomenon
a sign of the gods
a staple of fear.
but it's you
who made me into the goon
and you curse me
and you say im expensive
yet i've never spent a dollar in my life
nor a nickel
or a penny,
you've tried to rope me into your society
you want to press charges and sue.
but in reality i know you're simply jealous
you wish you could walk in my shoes,

you know that i cannot be moved
even if all the smartest people
conspired against me
and the strongest men and women were brought
together
even the superheroes cannot push me away.
i am vortex
i am a spinning psychotic madman
and that's the way i love it
i am tornado.

# Chapter IV

constellations were just distant light patterns
and then i met you
you pulled me so close
i could feel the star's hearts
exploding ever so slowly
so warmly.
you gave me a pattern
and called me beautiful
so beautiful.
you said
'this is your orbit, don't stray too far from
me'
and i didn't.
for my new orbit is perfect
as i circled you
i studied your smallest features
and fell in love
your big brown eyes
that watched me passionately
so passionately.
your gentle manner
so peaceful.
i said
'i could do this forever'
and i did.
for my new orbit became all i needed
time went on
and slowly more stars came around
they came to observe your light
so beautifully lit
some were magnificent themselves
and they could shine much brighter
than i could
so you looked through the lights
and you looked through the shadows
but in your searching
emerged a light even darker than i
he was big and had features
he had a large heart
and he gave it to you.
you readily took him in

and you found a perfect center stage orbit.
and now
i am on crash course.
i said
'Goodbye'
but you no longer listen.
for my orbit was taken
and i am left with nothing
but a burning core
my name is supernova.
but you can call me defeated
or loveless
or permanently dismembered,
call me lost
if i never get to love my bright sun.
though once i'm particles floating in the
galaxy
i pray they find their way back to you
so i can again see your beauty

# Chapter V

i promised to never write about it
and every time i placed my pen on the paper
creativity wouldn't follow.
i scoffed at my ventilation
at my emotional release of sputtered words
how idiotic a thing
a crush is
a parasitic dream that wastes no time
spreading disease and laying waste
to what you love
and only to make space for empty dreams
and thoughts of that person.
the more i think about it
the more confident i am that love
wasn't meant to be shared,
it wasn't meant for this
everlasting affair between two.
the more confident i become that love
shouldn't be sought after
at least not through connection.
maybe love was never meant to be more than
experience
maybe love shared through humanity
was an economic capitalization.
maybe i'm only saying all of this
because i drowned very deep in toxic water
water that poisoned my soul
torched my body
and torments my mind with horrific ghosts
that whisper soft insults
this is why i could never write about it
or should i say her
because her ghost lives
implanted in my brain
and wouldn't allow me
the opportunity to tell the world
how trapped i am,
in this grand scheme
this shouldn't be so important
this rejection
this obvious state of unloving imperfections

why do i dare let it abuse my mind.
because maybe i have it all wrong
maybe love is actually inevitable
maybe love turns out to be all you'll ever
truly need.
and maybe that kind of love
is only harvested through another person
and that loving interaction.
Regardless.. or rather
in conclusion
i am wrong
and if i'm right
i hope i'm wrong
maybe this life isn't worth living without
loving
perhaps that's why i died.
through the art of being forgotten
being a worthless contributor
to this grand scheme.
maybe i just didn't find my purpose soon enough
and i disappeared.
i'm sorry for the lack of absolutes
but i am dead,
and you will never know anything for certain
once you are nothing but a tablecloth
with some eye holes.
i am a ghost.
and my duty is to ponder
anything that i can
but i will never again know something for
certain
except that i still love you

# Chapter VI

it's hard to explain
why the heart wants certain things so
passionately
a musical tune
an animal
a person.
why be so drawn to objects
our mind always two steps behind
in pursuit of the evasive heart,
the heart so speedily chasing after things
charging with open arms
for it knows the name that quenches its spirit
and it sees that name
plastered on the walls
and etched onto the floors of the sewers.
it is my name
it's a name known by all
whether or not they take as much pleasure in it
as their heart does,
a box of chocolates can only half way promote
the name that is mine
but if you've truly felt my presence
it's a feeling you cannot easily forget.
i am warm
or refreshing cold
i am luminescent
i am harmonic
i am strings in staccato
or i roar in marvelous forte.
i am waves and the beaches they touch
i am bright green eyes
i am deeply thoughtful brown eyes
i am your favorite person,
i am your faithful four legged friend
i am the final topping on your favorite dessert
i am one of many forms
and places
and objects.
but i am so much more than that

for i am a deep sound reverberation
that stirs in your stomach,
i am a creator of chaos
even in the most subtle season,
for you find my name when
you are least looking to find it
like graffiti painted on the white house.
some who see that name will run in fear
some will hide their face
some will run towards
with open arms
only to see that it wasn't my name at all.
my name is easily disguised by other desires
some hidden so deeply in the heart
it is almost impossible to see through the
facade
for no matter how unimpressive
all turn their eyes to a firework.
all wish to run with the gazelles
all want their interior walls
to be branded
and seared by my name
for my name is love.
and i carry heavy weight
weight that not all can carry
but weight that all will try to.

# Chapter VII

i am always watching.
i have seen your every mistake
and i have made note of it
so as to never forget,
i fill your books
and one day your great great grandchildren
can open me up
and dig deep
into all your successful failures.
how humanity lost to the robotic race
how our climate died
before our very eyes
how even in our darkest moments
the human race refused to join together as a
whole.
how the nuclear warfare only made things worse
shocking
not shocking that in irony
a bomb could make a situation worse
but irony in that you've done it before.
humanity has managed to make me feel
so worthless
i am written record of what not to do
if nothing else,
and i stand by watching the same mistakes
made over
and over again.
why ?
because humanity is afraid of exploratory
failure
they'd rather fail over and over
in the same way
because it's at least expected
and it's familiar
it's nostalgic.
but in my books there comes days
when a call to action
becomes a necessity
and less a request,

and when that day comes
and the pioneers of the time
lift their war flags
the elders will stand against them
and claw
for as much of the old life
they can keep.
and the pioneers will continue to push for the
new
the better
the fair.
and i will stand by
and wait to record their success
and their eventual catastrophe
for all good comes to an end,
except for i
for i will never die.
i am history

# Chapter VIII

the mind of a clock is synchronized rhythm
tick followed by tock
tock followed by tick,
and at its heart is time
and for a clock to be happy
it can't be manipulated,
though giving your heart and love to time
is a dangerous game
it'll slow in the moments you wish it to tick
faster
and speed through times of love and happiness
time is the devil
that we wish to take control of.
for life is a series of tick tocks
that'll flash before you blink
it'll drain before you think
it'll dehydrate before you drink,
though the clock will continue on
every ding and every dong
a constant reminder that another second has
evaded your time.
to this moment
you've lost another to reading this
and another
and now another,
so on and so forth until you become panicked
there's only so many seconds you have remaining
it could be in the millions
it could be in the thousands.
so it does beg to ask hard questions
before the next tick
are you prepared to make a difference ?
can you free yourself from the sickness ?
how many bucket list items
have been checked from your checklist,
we're all spilt soda cans
trying to mop up our messes,
though in a world where mistakes are mistaken
as failures
perhaps our failures shouldn't be cleaned with
a mop,

perhaps we should throw a towel on top
and move on.
because when seconds are numbered
how many should you spend on things
you've already done
and how many should you spend on making new
ones,
going on midnight runs
or coming up with bad puns.
time is an evaluation of your dedication to be
an abomination
your dissatisfaction of the imagination of
important legion
and the slight fraction that tells the story of
you and your faction.
so in these seconds,
do you count ?
do you tick and tock
till your heart stops ?
so you're no better than your houses clocks
no better than the clicks as a door unlocks,
no better than the dog that chases the
invisible fox
we live in a paradox.
where time is so important
that we shouldn't pay attention to it,
if we did there would be no concentration
on infatuation with the numbered ticks left in
the ticker
clicks in the clicker.
your time could be long
and it could be short
it's not for you to decide.
treat every second the clock gives you
with deep enrichment
make differences
create reality.
most importantly
do what makes you happy,
tick followed by tock
tock followed tick
where's your life heading
before you hear

the next
click ?

- the clock

# Chapter IX

i am not a killer
i am a simple distraction
an action to certain reactions
a dissatisfaction
with current real imaginations.
a reality that's imaginary
you see a very real storm
and i'll tint it ten times as dark
you dream of a good time
and instead you run into a completely different
world
i make the world lethal.
but i don't kill
i just push you there
i tie knots in your stomach until you have no
hope of escaping the butterflies
i just dropped down there.
i make your head spin
i take your skin and i burn it
i shut your voice
i make your eyesight blur.
your fear of me only institutes me stronger
i only infiltrate your bones deeper
i spread like a plague
and stay long enough to destroy
any possible current pleasure.
don't dare cross me
i'll make you jittery.
i am on the offensive
and i can penetrate through the toughest
defenses,
though you
you are strong.
stronger than any i've come across
stronger than lots
for you've given up fighting back against me
but now i can't find a place
to instill my horror.
your mind is clear

your smile is carefree
your drive..
it's pure
i am a horrible figure
but i yield to those who are strongest
i prefer to feed on the week
i have no time to give you
i am anxiety
but you've repelled my attacks..
today

# Chapter X

i've watched you cry for so very long
and it breaks me to see you
so deeply rooted into this funk
your old ways have become ancient tactics
in this modern world
they have failed you.
i watch helplessly
as instead of turning to me
you push on with your failed routines
they're all you ever learned.
fear stands between your way to feeling better
but it bears more sinister criminals
than you can fight alone
anxiety
depression
feeling hopeless
all worshipers and faithful servants
to the monsters you fight daily.
and you haven't launched an offensive yet
your cagematch with letting go of the old
the harm
it still rages on,
you sit and think about her all day
endlessly
even though you know you are at best a distant
memory
visited on occasion in her mind
why ?
it's time to stick up a finger
and shout profanities to those that wronged you
it's time to break free.
take my hand
i will show you how to push
how to forget
how to keep living
maybe even smile
with genuine intention
from time to time
what a thought..
but without me

you will be stuck as you.
broken
empty
confused.
together
and together only
can we start again.
beginning with a chapter to be closed
a freshness to be awakened
a sacrifice of your old broken soul
the sight of a future or purpose
and the breath of a giant
just coming to life
ready to show
the world can't keep you down.
my name is new.
and i grant second chances
and thirds
and fourths
if need be.
for i am limitless
just as we are,
together

# Broken Romantic Schematics

broken romantic schematics,
you told her you loved her
long before you ever felt it.
broken romantic schematics,
you took her home
before you took her to dinner.
broken romantic schematics,
let alone the fact that you've dated
hundreds of guys
you always end up pulling away
because you're afraid to fully commit and be
rejected.
so you love half heartedly,
display only enough interest to keep that lover
on the line,
but everyday you wake
you think about how he or she is the wrong one,
a broken scheme.
these schemes never justified the means,
you'll always end up heartbroken,
always end up unfulfilled.
you've forgotten how it feels,
to have love on your side.
to be cared for by someone willingly.
so i ask you,
how much longer can you keep this act up ?
how long until you drown so deep
in the schematic you become another player
in the game.
will you ever realize there's better ways,
better people,
better love.
will you dare to break your schemes,
in the name of love.
real love.

# dagger my heart till i stop breathing

the sad truth is
i love you.
i don't want to
i shouldn't need to
but i do.
and i hate it
because it feels like
you are capable
of loving everyone else
besides me,
you love him
him
and him
but you can't love me.
and somewhere below my twisted knot stomach
and butterflies in my gut
i understand.
but i can't stop loving you
i love you with every ounce
every inch
and every brain cell.
with every pump of blood
the vessels chant your name
like a sports fan proclaims
love for their favorite players.
but it's evident enough
you play for another team
and i am done fighting for your attention
i'm tired of foraging through your forests
and flower beds for an engraving of my name,
i've had enough of the sickness in my stomach
the long nights with long tears
that drip slowly down my cheeks
and dampen my chin.
the lost breath in my lungs
the numbness in my fingertips
the headache that never goes away.
so i ask of you
the biggest favor
and it comes with a gift,

a dagger.
and if you could be so kind
as to place it's jagged edges
so profoundly through my arteries
piercing my scalp
inside my lungs.
stab with passion
stab with intent to kill
never stop stabbing
until you've taken every last breath.
it's not fair
it's nobody's fault
but still that feels like i'm losing
a lost battle.
so stab away
this pain has entered my soul
and i won't stand to see myself
break over another human
no matter how great they are
and you are truly spectacular,
i just wish i never touched your flame
for i've been on fire
for longer than i can remember
and you stood by holding the extinguisher,
but never put me out.
you couldn't see my torched wounds
you burned through the deepest layers of skin
leaving me with my outer shell
and nothing beneath it.
so stab away,
my bonfire
and in my dying moments i'll whisper to you
i love you.
and you'll realize that no matter how hard you
try
no matter how big the crime
there's nobody else
who i'd bear to stand by.

## your smile

a constant reminder of why i love you
seeing your lips curl upwards
the dimples exposed
the way your eyes
squint just a pinch.
my soul is restored
if only for a brief fleeting moment
i feel warm
i feel cold
i feel alive.
even though
you just killed everything in my body
i reach out from inside
trying to feel your soul
and once that smile
paints your face
i know i can feel your genuinity
your honest deep happiness
makes my heart cry
producing the happiest tears of joy.
i make effort
to bring that smile around
and it's a never ending endeavor to see it
if just once more,
a perfect drug
that i am forever addicted to.
the day that smile is not my daily privilege
will be the same day
my soul is silenced.
the same day my pen
can't reach paper
the moment when i'll never
be fine again.
and it feels as though
it's approaching all too fast.
these days i still see that smile
but more and more infrequently
by my own doing,
i see that smile when your with others
forced to watch from a distance

where i feel it less.
until eventually
seeing it means almost nothing
if nothing
then pain.
i am burning to feel your soul reach back
when mine reaches out.
that's when i realized
your smile isn't mine to keep
and you realized
that i am just a freeloader,
a thief who sneaks into the movie theater
a sad impersonation of a heart speaker.
i miss that smile
i miss that face
i think about it often
i just hope one day
it will dawn on me again.

# the fog

this long beach i walk
but my eyes stay fixed behind me
unable to look at what's to come
only on what we lost.
the fog that chases me
hiding everything i could've seen
the sand i walk on
becomes heavier than ever.
with every moment i look behind,
quick sand wraps my ankles to a choke hold
the fog moves in
and along with it my diminishing chances
to see something new
or to feel something
that's not bleak
to start over
to move on.
in the fog
i feel you more than ever
it's where we first met
our bond built strong by broken bounds
and i past on my many chances to live under
clearer skies
in hopes we would leave the fog together still
but fog burns.
we burned
and it feels so stupid
we had all this water available
to smother what was on fire
but we never did
we kind of enjoyed how it hurt.
i can't see you in this new fog
but i know you're here,
the echo of waves crashing
send shivers down my spine
they speak to me
telling of missed chances
love lost
love that was never supposed to be.
quicksand now neck high

and moving fast
i can finally turn my head forward,
for it no longer shows the future
but what could've been.
a beautiful sunset over the oceanside
a lady who sits on the beach
watching all alone
the one she was supposed to love,
was taken by the fog.
and now for my failure
the fog moves towards her too

# a plea to those watching over us

if you are out there
watching and listening,
to the boy sitting on the rooftop
watching the sun fall
humming so softly
simple soft tears dropping quietly
down his cheeks,
a broken mess at best.
for he so wants nothing more but happiness,
and he doesn't even care if it's something he
ever reaches,
this happiness he yearns for isn't for himself,
it's for someone he loves.
with deep passion,
even when her passions are so different.
he's listened and walked for years,
watching her display firework shows
for three hundred and sixty degree displays
that don't bat an eye his way.
little did she know he would count himself
blessed to see just a single firecracker.
and he would watch her,
as she tore herself to pieces,
belabored her spirit,
spat on her own face and disgraced her name,
all because she believed she wasn't good enough
for love,
when mr. love was next to her the whole time.
his timidness prevented him from going for it,
her brokenness making her blind to his shy
hints,
and now time intervenes.
time views this as sad and cringful and
declares no more.
so she went to a far away place,
he stayed home,
collecting scraps of dust and dirt
that he used to remember what's left of her.

he sits on the rooftop and thinks of her soft
voice,
thinks of her differences from everyone else,
thinks of those perfect eyes.
and he weeps.
and if anyone is looking down from above,
they may shed a tear as well,
for this,
is brokenness.

# new blood

my heart does more
than beat
for every full pulsation
there's a strong recurring vibration
sending earthquake level shaking
inside my body and bones.
every vibration makes my fists clench
my muscles tense
and my body becomes drenched
in your blood.
the vibrations echo
through all that's hollow
the screams of your horrors,
somehow they've found a new home here.
perhaps your soul is finally dead
maybe you've just given up hope
maybe i was the last one
before you're truly forgotten.
my veins ache
and though my mind is dormant
my soul keeps it awake.
for the sunday morning cartoons are on
and they all feature you.
they all feature the smeared decapitation
of our long lasting seared reputation
of being top dogs in this population
and the revitalization
of only half of our plans to be everyone's
favorite fascination.
for you and i just became
you in i
your love runs dry
my love runs fluently
but without a winner
my heart remains a carnival prize,
i'm tired of carrying your extra weights
that remind me i can't be great
and that my pure hate
is embodied inside of me and my ugly.

i'm tired of things being this way
i want new blood to take me
and circulate me.
i need a breath of that fresh air
that makes me feel care free,
i want to inhale the salty air of the sea
until my nose is salty enough to serve on
dinner table dishes
i need an iv bag to replenish me with a new
stream
one that doesn't know your name.
for no matter how hard i try
the blood cells reproduce
and reform back into the shapes
that spell your name
here i sit
and wait for a change
and sitting has never changed anything
maybe that's exactly the point.

# broken nights

on this broken night
i look upwards,
i hope to see some clarity
i hope to hear glistening from shiny stars
i hope to feel some peace
in seeing that there are other stars
in the sky.
but i see none alone in the night sky
you shine so bright and bold
i could swear you stole an angel's halo,
i scour the night sky
for the faintest glow of another
but they don't show.
my eyes so trained on your beauty
that i forget that the rest of the sky carries
others
i forget that i'm not the only one
who watches you
i forget that no matter what i do
you'll never see me the way
i want you to.
and even if you did
it'd be a fool's mission to pursue what love
we could've had
our astronomical paths
simply fail to cross
in ways that would be compatible.
so don't shine on me any longer
my soul poisoned by your warmth
my heart broken by your glow
my eyes so hesitant to move on
but they must,
there's bound to be others
though i know it'll be long
before i accept that.
there may not be brighter than her
but there's a chance,
and a chance at happiness
is more powerful than to fall

into a life of sadness.
to all the other stars
that hide in front of me
glow strong and bright,
for this world gets cold alone
and it only gets colder
with each day.

# a final schematic

if you still don't know how to love
after all you've read
i'd say the answer is very clear
dear reader,
don't.
do not.
quit while you are ahead.
and not beaten to a pulp by yourself.
over the could have's
and the never will be's
over the lost forever's
and the keepers that were unkept.
don't play this game,
there is no happy end
no victories
no rewards
only brutal blows
low kicks
and sudden sharp jabs
that cut through more than flesh.
though the harsh truth
in reality
is that
we'll never stop.
we are human
and love will follow us
for love
loves to win
we are
it's easy prey.
it doesn't matter
how hard it hits
we reset
and we want more
with every failure
an increase in need.
and if we are to play this torture filled game
we may as well try and win,
so go
go talk to her
until you find yourselves to be

incompatible.
go tell him
you're attracted to him
until he tells you he has a type
or more likely,
until you realize
he's an asshat.
remember to remember who you are
and what you stand for
for that's who is playing the game
not your body.
remember that this game
has tricks
and don't let yourself become one,
be careful who you play this game with
and most importantly,
don't let it consume you.
games are fun
so is life
if you let it.
don't forget how unserious everything is
when you're busy being unserious about
everything.
don't dagger your heart
it's not worth it,
this game will hurt you enough.
don't think of that smile if it's truly your
world ender.
erase those worst horror stories
and move into your new brightly lit kingdom,
and don't plea to those who watch us
if they're going to respond
why not make your words count..
and if your blood echoes names
maybe all you need is a doctor to look at that.
this is your final schematic
on this very broken night
go and love.
and then break
and fall apart.
repiece
and find peace
until it cycles over again.

until the cycle breaks
once and for all

# The Others

## Court Jester

i am an undertaking
for all my years in my king's service
never did i receive the attention
that i obtain now.
a walking joke
a staple in self depreciation,
every street i walk
my manner itself filters in humor
to the eyes of thy bypassers.
even the squires acknowledge me
as nothing
but the fool.
what this kingdom doesn't know
behind each joke
is a little truth.
i never meant it to get to this
i have a knights heart
don't i ?
have i told myself lies
for so long ?
if i have
why do i carry on ?
what's my heart's song ?
what do i love anymore ?
i've come to a place
where my only attention
is stupidity driven humor.
not all the blame is mine
this world swallows pity laughter
by the gallon full,
though when i stand before the king
i don't hesitate to crack egg shell
after egg shell
onto my cranium.
i do not stop

until tears are dropped from the faces
until knees are slapped
it's not an act
that i want to do,
i chase glory.
i seek the love of true lovers
but i sit here
juggling knives that cut at my throat
and my lungs
trying to choke out what little humanity
i still cling to.
how long can one keep this act up
for one day
i'll say a thing that's not so funny,
my truly sad and disgraced colors
will make an appearance in the courts
of my kings and queens,
and they'll call for my throat.
show business brings no real friends
yet i keep this act up
clinging to the only real appreciation i
receive,
even if it's
for being an idiot.

# a flutter

i love you
i always have
i figured i'd never stop
until i stood in front of a train
and was hit so hard
my head fell off..
but i had a flutter
nothing too prolonged
nothing too obvious
would've missed it completely
if i wasn't standing perfectly still.
something that happened
only in the heart,
a quick off pace beat from the rhythm i've
become accustomed to
something stopped for just but half of a moment
but it made me think
out of all the things to stop happening for a
half of a moment what could it be ?
could it just be nothing ?
if it was just nothing
why didn't all things happen the same ?
perhaps there was no flutter at all
maybe i made that flutter up
to tell myself something
to bring notice to an evil
i don't want to accept.
this flutter could just be a nudge
to point me back to the right direction.
but then again
it could just be an irregularity of my heart
beat,
a sign of a potential problem down the road.
it did hurt
though it was so short
i was alright within moments
so why is my mind sore for hours ?
im going to forget about it now
because now it all seems so worthless..
not speaking about the flutter
but about this relationship.

## falling in love with red, when your favorite color is blue

the human race is an infinite canvas
waiting infinitely for colors to change them,
when paint is slinged
stroked
dashed
and flung onto our paint boards and sketchbooks
the conclusion is a painting.
whether symbolic of good or bad
subtle or outlandish
or something vague
like love and sorrow
that painting is what assembles
who we are.
it tells our stories
without words,
my painting is all blues
grays
blacks
and whites.
though this abstract spray painted canvas isn't
much,
it is me.
and through trial and failure
everytime i dropped it into the street
everytime i tried to paint over it
everytime i buried it into the sand
it stays the same.
for it is me
some other color has always existed
though you can't see it on the surface
you have to look inside.
a burgundy splatter mark.
blue is my favorite color
though there lies something so entirely
different
so unfortunately close.
if this color was seen on the surface
it would be judged harshly
what an odd placement

into an otherwise color graphically
pleasing piece.
what a sour show to a subtle song
what a great disruption from a gracious wave
they'd pick apart burgundy
until they run out of gas and hit the wall
never bearing a glance
at my endless pitch blacks
or blinding bright whites.
this burgundy burden buries my body and breaks
my bones
and it didn't stop
until it had my soul,
it's a curse
but all curses are good magic tricks
by entities with strong forceful power.
and who doesn't like some magic ?
it's a life instiller
a saturationist
an abolishing of dull and dreary.
so i turned my cheek
i embrace my red
and my awkward outstanding.
i'm ready for the world to love me for my red
and my blue
for my whites
and my blacks
for my brights
and my blands
for my canvas
just as it stands

# nobody to fill the void

it's come to this
though i wish my heart would've realized sooner
the deep dark pit
the darkness that spreads
it's not meant to be buried by dirt.
nor is it meant to be filled by love
love is the great lie
when you think love
you think of her
of him
of it
of this
of that
when you think love
you think possession.
love is an action
it's not a game or a race
it's a dance,
a dance with fire
a dance in nature
a dance of promising never to promise
it's a reminder that uncertainty
is the only certainty.
it tells us that history reports of many
people
who lived fabulous lives alone,
do not shed tears
for the people who aren't with you
to dance by the fire,
do not cry for the ones
that departed to the red sun
or for those who hide from you
on the darkest piece of the moon
and never forget to run far from the wolves
who get hungry over time,
never forget that love is a binding
a persuasive allusion
a necessity
that's also a distraction
never stop dancing

until the northern lights fill your memory
don't stop singing
until the biggest waves
swallow the sun whole
and don't stop playing
till you're certain you've loved this world
as much as it wants to love you.
breathe until you've proven yourself good at
it,
then you can finally show others
what you've done so well.

# Something Beautiful

please let me write something beautiful
something that reminds me
there's still good in the world
some things that show us
that we're still worth fighting for.
i just want to write something worth writing
something free of sadness
free of shame
free of madness
free of hate
free of obligations
and free,
of course.
something full of love
full of peace
full of fun
something to shout high above
something full of joy
filled with hugs
something to shut them up
to shut them down
to make them rough
for their angry hearts
don't deserve my art
now they are left in the..
and once again my dominant emotions were led
i'm left feeling cold
and empty
do i truly feel nothing
but how to be angry ?
why is it that the only peace i can feel
is the piece i have sucked from someone else's
soul.
i am terribly terribly terrible
i am horribly horribly hateful
i am fearfully fearfully fearful
that i am locked in a simulated paradoxically
created world
where i play the villain.
now i've reached my limits

i've drawn myself so far away from where i was
in the beginning
where has the love gone ?
where is the peace ?
can you ever truly feel peace
or feel at ease
without the true answer
for the sole location of the deceased ?
so i'll continue to travel further west
of the entirety of humanity's biggest damn mess
for my peace lies
i feel most of my peace staring in the big
green eyes
of the giant in size.
what i'm really trying to say is
the only true peace is
we're fucked till the lines gone
we're fucked till the times gone
fucked till the sun eats us alive.
there's nothing peaceful about oblivion,
but it sure as hell looks beautiful.

## no control

whether or not there's an actual cliff i've
slipped off of
i know i've fallen from something
or at least some bit of me has.
maybe murder .

maybe suicide
i no longer can tell the difference
and i'm done investigating
what's the point of discovering
a mystery's heart,
if you're falling through the air.
it was suicide
i pushed myself off that cliff
i was so tired of holding myself up so high
that i cut my ties and asked to die
i'm tired of holding myself
to such high standards
living the way i thought would please you
and show me as a man of character
if i'm a character
this week i'll be stupid as a donkey
and next week as drunk as a rich homeless man
and the following as sexually promiscuous
as a broke prostitute.
i'm done being the good guy
everyone loves a good idiot
it's time to discover that piece of myself
that inner idiot.
it's time to piss on graves
and shit on my dreams
it's time to throw unnecessary punches
and shave the mouths of those
who helped me fall from this high place.
i know how stupid this sounds
but that's exactly the point.
the idiotic
consider taking life seriously
to be psychotic.
here i am
not sure how to escape the middle
of being a deep thinker

and wanting to be dumb as nails.
it's time to think deeply
about how to stop thinking so deep,
i say all of this
while my heart feels broken
give me a few weeks
and i'll look back at who wrote this
and shake my head.
life is progression
desaturation and then resaturation
declination and then inclination
life and then
death.

# times get dark

times get dark
and we start to cling
we cling
to what we think we want and need.
we cling because metallic bond is stronger
than the new severed human connection,
it's escape
from the mind's dark monster resurrection.
you feel him holding your shoulders from behind
he lets you spend all the time you need
pretending he's not there
but you both know at some point
you will run out of distractions
and you'll have to face him.
times get dark
and we start to run
we run to places we feel safe
we run because running
is all we've ever known.
there's no true safety in our running
but it feels as though
we might run into our nirvana
like a transparent brick wall
on the middle of a sidewalk.
we run to alcohol
we run to pills
we run to mental starvation
we run to bad relationships
we may as well run to suffocation.
i have not written in quite a while
it's hard to write on the run
but perhaps,
i should just stop in my tracks
perhaps whatever i thought was pursuing me gave
up
long ago.
maybe the chaos of breaking down inside and
out
shouldn't be run from,
but rather embraced as a fact of life

as an irreversible step that may fly you
to who you are supposed to become one day
to who you'll be for the rest of your life.

# embrace the chase

is it writers block
if the block doesn't stop moving ?
transformations and reconfigurations
unscrambling and rescrambling the unscrambled
scraps and sheets,
we've all cleaned out a dirty closet
cluttered by clothes in pursuit of that one
shirt
and as i search through my dirty cluttered
brain
i'm looking for something harder to find than
any pair of pants.
a feeling and an action,
i continuously place pen in hand and ink on
paper
and fail to write what i mean to translate
i continuously paint pictures
that are uninteresting,
and i know that's because
i avoid the messy closet
the dark in my heart.
trying to organize this messy clutter
trying to put up the broken shelves is
sometimes an inescapable truth we have to live
with,
and it strangles our lungs
breaks our arms
it antagonizes our anxieties
it asks how much do we value that shirt truly.
sometimes the easiest way to cope
is to set fire to closet
to turn your back on everything
even yourself
because who you are has nothing to do with what
you've done
but is solely dependent on who you wake up as
tomorrow.
the past is for others to judge you
the future is for you to change them
or forget them

or disappear completely.
so i stripped the shirt off my back
and threw it into the bonfire
that once was a messy closet.
now i find myself a clean slate
new music to taste
new clothes to experiment
new people to dance with
new words to place on paper.
for in this recession of writing
in these dark ages
you rediscover yourself
in ways you weren't expecting
but once you find yourself again
you can restore life to breath
and restore breath to your breath.
as you stand in the ashes
don't recollect what you left behind
it's transformed just as you did,
that mess became ash
you became naked and new
embrace the chase.

# <u>Letters From the Heart, Brain, and Soul</u>

## brain to heart 1

despite our best trying efforts
to avoid falling into the same pits as the
average man
the pits stands before us.
and it's darker than we imagined
it's deeper than our deepest most hopeless
dreams
it stretches as far as is visible with the
mind's eye
and it's moving.
encroaching on our ability to move forward
at least
to do so happily
we could press on into this dark night
but seeing in darkness was never something we
were very good at
and we've been trying for so long already,
navigating these unexplored maps and backwards
compasses make traversing this strange world
we've been building harder and harder to push
progress.
the nerves are feeling something new,
it feels a bit like a white flag,
our enemies feel so much bigger and stronger
than our defenses can hold
so maybe diving into this pit head first is the
easiest way to cope.
but maybe it'll make everything worse
perhaps that pits floor is laced with sickles,
spearheads, and bear traps,
ready to stab, slice, and force fatality.
we know who put these pits in front of us,
we know to fall in is giving them another

victory,
so why do i ask you to jump in ?
have i become addicted to feeling pain ?
do i wish for terrible inflictions to be
sustained in our soulbody ?
i can no longer know,
the poor soul has taken such vigorous torturing
for lengths longer then we bare to keep track
of,
and who's to really say how many more punches
he can take.
we've almost lost him
you and i both know,
the sparseness of writings,
the change in tone, music taste, ideals,
this pit is no pit at all but a lake
a lake black as midnight
so dark its liquid doesn't feel wet
so cold it's form disturbs the entire body upon
the slightest touch
and it's poison so intoxicating,
so deceiving,
you find yourself three feet deep before you've
moved a foot.
to you heart i just ask an impossible question,
what is your greatest desire ?
what makes your beats happiest,
what makes the blood warm ?
and how do we restore raging fire to the veins
instead of this lukewarm bullshit that moves
so  lazily throughout my bloodstream.
so many paths,
but so many of them just end up in this pit.
please heart.. is this our fate..
or is this our final failure.
perhaps surrendering our current
will benefit our deeper longevity,
but who's to say if our soul will ever climb
it's way back out.
and death by suffocation would only be the
worst way to go.

# heart to brain 1

it's been long since we spoke.
our indifferences have lead to these current
consequences,
our past decisions and missed consultations
dropped us in this very pit,
though our past is sad and it pulls me down,
i know you are the one that ultimately controls
when we frown.
so i ask why are we pursuing the place we most
dread ?
a place where monsters lurk around every
corner,
a place that'll remind us we're nothing but
foreigners,
a place that'll torture and sour what we stand
for,
a place that embodies the system we wish to
demolish.
this is no question,
this is no great pondering like our pure days
in the past,
this is real life suicide.
you control the legs,
remove us from this wasteland,
never look back on it.
our home is far far away,
a place by the ocean don't you remember ?
in our bamboo structure ?
with the beaches and the sun
where we can remember all that we've overcome.
to pioneer,
to adventure,
to become the one who is apart of nature.
this lake we sit in damages my bloodstream..
get out of it.

# brain to heart 2

at what point have we gone too far ?
at what point do we face the music that all
that we've built up for is stupid in
conclusion,
beating a system that's built on delusion will
not stop our frustration.
we have to walk on these paths and we can't
regret each step we take,
this war was lost many generations before we
ever had the chance to step in and make our own
messy cake,
now we are force fed this curriculum,
this circumstance,
but where we must thrive is on where we take
our stance,
all is not lost dear heart though i know it
feels so much like it,
there's still a chance to hold onto our soul in
this dark pit,
because if it's a pit we may just fall deeper
and farther through an abyss which means we
currently aren't on the bottom.
and if we aren't yet there who's to say there
isn't a grand trampoline waiting to take use
our downward spiral and turn it back into
something miraculous.
we will very rarely agree on anything,
but let's try and agree on this,
for our soul.
for our body.
for me.
for you.

# heart to brain 2

yet what's the need for a trampoline if you've
never started falling ?
so naive is the mind that thinks falling deeper
into darkness,
will have opportunity to end with kindness.
so cynical the idea to torture in free spirit,
this is why the soul has gone so unspoken,
grown so disconnected.
he was pushed out and replaced by broken
feelings,
stupid songs and ideas with no true purpose or
meaning.
you've become very quick to turn your back on
what we've built towards,
this world is only our oyster when we can make
it so,
this traveling spirit of ours will have to be
silenced and suspended,
we will have to keep breathing that toxic air,
how i miss that natural smell.
don't forget the smell of pine,
that pure mountain air,
that fresh ocean breeze,
the softness of sand,
the cooling of a nice seattle rain,
and the soul's smile on a san diego sunset.
where we will go the soul will only cry so
don't say it's for the best for him,
or for the body that's surely in for a rude
awakening,
or for me,
i'll only bleed more.

## soul to brain & heart

no longer will you need to speak for me,
i have awaken from my hibernation to a
situation that does nothing but push us to a
final decision.
i see two clear choices,
and no clear winners.
two very different paths,
but no real certainties.
i would argue that each could be equally
beneficial,
yet either could be equally dissatisfactory.
you often refer to me as if im a whole entity
alone,
though i am not.
we are two.
and we feel different things,
we see through different eyes and hear through
other ears.
i see how beautiful our adventures out in the
world could be
but i also see how maybe just what we need is a
new community
and to play a little hockey.
i do miss the smell of pine,
but i also miss the warmth of human flesh,
i haven't been felt in far too long,
i haven't been acknowledged in even longer.
maybe there's another soul who needs a hug,
and who's really to say where that will be
a path less traveled
or the one traveled by all.
all i know is we must all work together to find
the answer,
the last thing we'd want to do is shoot deep
into the dark,
and kill somebody.

# Outro Shots

## 100 poems

one hundred poems ago
i didn't think i was very good at anything
one hundred poems ago
my outlook on life was so very dark
so impossibly beautiful.
one hundred poems ago
i thought the most beautiful thing life
could offer was wealth
so much has changed.
so much potential has blossomed
so much youthfulness was left behind
to chase something much bigger.
through poetry came an outlet
a vessel to transpose a deep embedded feeling,
an ember
or rather a spark
something that flickered when i turned it on
something that i long ago
tried to bury in hopes that it wasn't who i
was.
but now i embrace it fully
i feel i can see the world differently from the
status quo.
i can focus on the minute
i can see poetry hidden in obvious places.
and yes i am very bad at most everything i do
i am a poor worker
sometimes a very poor friend
and a socially uncomfortable specimen
to be gathered near
but i do blame it all on my thoughts.
for they are rabbit trails and portals
that all lead towards things
that usually are not only irrelevant but
pointless.
though sometimes
they blossom.

they become so dangerously deep
that if not careful
they can suffocate you.
and then they become one of these 100
i am very proud of myself
and i may be the only one
and i'm more than okay with that.
for my world can stay overly beautiful and
overly saturated
and i can stay satisfied
with the rare filter that covers my lens.
and in the end
i am happy
i know i will write more and more
until one day the pen finally is retired
and the journal is forever shut.

# I Want To Love You
to the earth i bring my nose
to the wind i put my ear
to the snow i bring my lips
i am helpless.

as poetry breathes,
i share a question.
the air that fills the space between you and i
and how i can push through it.
the heavy air that presses in my chest every
time i whisper your name.
the sweet taste of your smile, the sweet
fireworks and sparks
that take me up and took my heart.
like a wave to be reckoned with,
like a song that sings of second chances,
i want to love you till there's nothing left
between us.
like an ocean spills into our minds,
let there be nothing left but love in our
lives,
i want to love you till there's nothing left
between us.
through the storms and it's deadly rage,
i will write of you page by page
till there's not a book left that isn't echoing
your name
as we grow old over time, our love will grow
forever prime,
i will love you to, the very end of the line.
like a beautiful newborn babies song,
i'll give you everything ive got,
i want to love you till there's nothing left
between us.
i want to love you till there's nothing left
between us.
i will love you till there's nothing left
within me.
you can count on me.
you can believe in me.
you will see me, forever building, forever

singing, forever being,
being in love with you.

## Outro

another journey through the mind
another chance to be kind
another light to find.
never stop reading
never stop loving
never stop breathing.
so here we are at the end
here we are ready to start again
here we must depart
but i'll join you again
this breath is dead
let the next one begin.

## a stubborn poem refusing to be categorized..

that's right bitch i don't fit into your little
'plan'.
i'm my own entity
i say what i want to say
which is whatever the hell i feel at the time
any filter you use to filtrate my unfertilized
version
of chaotic commotion
will be ruined by my vicious brutality
and reckless rage.
you think i belong in 'wild' ?
im twice as wild as your wildest dream
and more motivated than any moving piece
in that shit show
you say it's not really a broken romantic piece
and you'd be right
my name is a stubborn asshole.
oops i told you that too early
guess that's not my home
at least not this christmas.
im a cynical bastard looking to aggravate the
youth
stir emotionally there elderly
twist the middle age into a terminal degrade.
and you all envy me
because i've managed to live outside the box
and make it look so easy.
and those that aren't envious
are the same ones who drink their tea and
coffee casually ogling their sexy barista
only paying me half the attention i rightfully
deserve
you boring shit bag
go write 150 shades of blue for all i care.
or the middle class who shit their pants
because i gave them a shoutout.
don't look at the damn notification on your
phone,
i'm not done speaking to you.

don't answer that doorbell,
i haven't finished ramming your brain
into your kneecap.
keep your eyes focused on the fire,
keep your hands clenched around my wrath,
keep your ass planted wherever you can get a
good view of what true power really looks like.
i'm the one who can't be categorized,
i'm the one whose job
is to keep getting in trouble with everyone
else.
i do nothing every year
but piss people off
it's a full time tilt
and you aren't wearing your helmet yet.
you're defenseless and im carrying an axe,
who comes out on top do you think ?
now bow down to your new king,
bow down to this fucking stubborn poem.

# The Poetry Book II

- Poetical Alphabet

- The Wild Returns

- NewKeepers

- My Name Is...

- Broken Romantic Schematics

- The Others

- Letters from the Heart, Brain, and Soul

- Outro Shots